Over 50 WAYS
– TO LEAVE –
YOUR LOVER

(with style)

Over 50 WAYS
~ TO LEAVE ~
YOUR LOVER
(with style)

COMPILED BY GEORGINA HARRIS

DESIGNED BY DAVID FORDHAM

CICO BOOKS
LONDON NEW YORK

Published in 2009 by CICO Books
An imprint of
Ryland Peters & Small
20–21 Jockey's Fields   519 Broadway, 5th Floor
London WC1R 4BW   New York, NY 10012

www.cicobooks.com

10 9 8 7 6 5 4 3 2 1

Design and illustrations © CICO Books 2009

A CIP catalog record for this book is available from the Library of
Congress and the British Library.

ISBN-13: 978 1 906094 89 8

Printed in China

Illustrator: Trina Dalziel

CONTENTS

Introduction

*H*ARD, SOFT, CRUNCHY, or with a melting middle? Like our favorite chocolate, break-ups come in all sorts of different shapes and sizes—and just like candy, no one wants to be the first to pick from the box.

But sometimes you have to make the first move—and this book shows you how. Whether you're slowly beginning to realize that your relationship is looking a touch last season, or that your lover treats his favorite sports team with more respect, these pages show you how to make the break.

Momentous life events deserve to be treated with style—after all, you look good, so why shouldn't you treat your inner self with the same respect and dazzling detail? Through the ages, poets, philosophers, and divas have thought the same and produced ways to move away with grace and glamor. In a collection ranging from wise words to poignant poetry and killer lines, you'll find the right way to let him go—and all the healing and hope you need to move on.

66The stylish woman never drinks and dials after a break-up.99

"I'm going to SMILE and make you think I'm HAPPY, I'm going to laugh, so you don't see me CRY, I'm going to let you go in *style*, and even if it kills me—I'm going to SMILE."

ANONYMOUS

8

Chapter 1

SAYING IT
WITH A

SMILE

"Marriage is a **GREAT** *institution*, but I'm not ready for an *institution* yet.**"**

MAE WEST (1893–1980)

Marriage
is a *wonderful* **invention;**
then again, **so is**
a bicycle repair kit.**"**

Attributed to **BILLY CONNOLLY** (1942–)

"If he was *dumb enough* to

LEAVE,

be *smart enough* to let him

WALK.**"**

ANONYMOUS

" *Oh,* LIFE is a glorious cycle of song,
A medley of extemporanea;
And LOVE is a thing that can never go wrong;
And *I am Marie of Romania.* **"**

DOROTHY PARKER Not So Deep as a Well (1893–1967)

12

> *You know how I end relationships?*
> *I don't say, "This isn't working out" or*
> *"I don't want to see you anymore."*
> *If I never want to see a man again*
> *I say, "You know, I love you.*
> *I want to marry you.*
> *I want to have your children."*
> *Sometimes they leave skidmarks.*

RITA RUDNER (1953–)

No time to make the break?...

DEAR SIR,

FOLLOWING YOUR recent application, I regret to inform you that you have not been selected as a final candidate for interview for the position of my partner.

The level of applications for the post was very high and many, indeed hundreds of, well-qualified candidates have not been successful at this time. As part of the policy of continuous monitoring and improvement currently in operation, the following performance feedback is provided for your benefit:

FINANCIAL ABILITIES. Your generous support of many small specialist distilleries may provide a selfless boost to commerce in our fine country, but buying me one drink would have counted too.

EMOTIONAL SUPPORT SKILLS. You're "aware," "sensitive," and "engaged." I'm "neurotic." Of course.

... *Do it by mail*

HOMEMAKING MANAGEMENT. Delegation isn't always the right answer.

LOYALTY. Being peeled off my best friend last week wasn't ideal. I've got jeans with more stretch than your version of the facts.

TEAMWORK. "What are you doing on Valentine's Day?" will never be an effective approach to any girlfriend.

HYGIENE AND APPEARANCE. No couch was meant to crunch. Leather jackets that stand up alone are unsanitary. As it happens, so is drooling at other women.

Thank you for your application. With all best wishes for success in your future romantic career,

YOURS SINCERELY,

"The only time a woman really succeeds in changing a man is when he's a baby."

NATALIE WOOD (1938–1981)

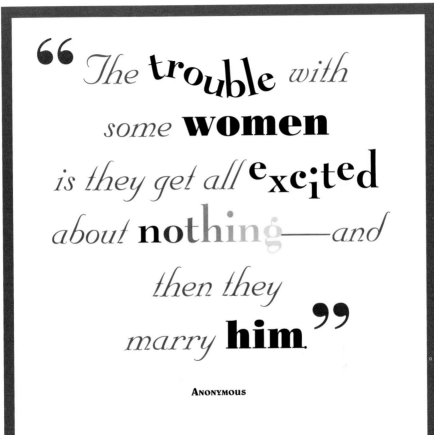

66 *The* **trouble** *with some* **women** *is they get all* **excited** *about* **nothing**—*and then they* **marry** **him**. **99**

ANONYMOUS

" **I** love to shop after a **bad** relationship. **I** buy a new outfit and it makes **me** feel **better**. Sometimes, if **I** see a really great outfit, **I**'ll **break up** with **someone** on purpose. "

RITA RUDNER (1953–)

Chapter 2

IT'S
SAD
BUT IN A
GOOD WAY

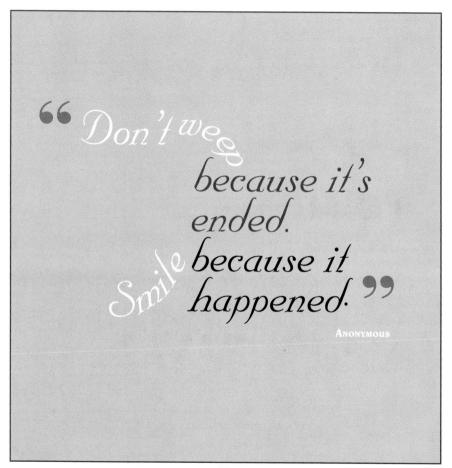

"Don't weep because it's ended. Smile because it happened."

ANONYMOUS

" **Hearts will NEVER BE PRACTICAL until they are made UNBREAKABLE.** "

THE WIZARD OF OZ (1939)
written by **NOEL LANGLEY** (1911–1980), **FLORENCE RYERSON**
(1892–1965), and **EDGAR-ALLAN WOOLF** (1881–1948)

21

"I don't
miss my man;
miss my man;
miss my man;
miss my man;

I miss the man
miss the man
miss the man
miss the man

I thought he was."

"Marriage is a misteake every girl should make."

" Friendship is certainly the *finest* balm for the pAngs of disappointed love. "

JANE AUSTEN (1775–1817)

"One must not tie a ship to a single anchor, nor life to a single hope."

EPICTETUS (55–135 CE)

"The day you end your old relationship is the first day you start building the love you deserve."

ANONYMOUS

love
love
love
love
love
love love love
love love love

"**I**T TAKES A MOMENT TO SAY *hello,* **BUT AN AGE TO SAY** *goodbye*."

ANONYMOUS

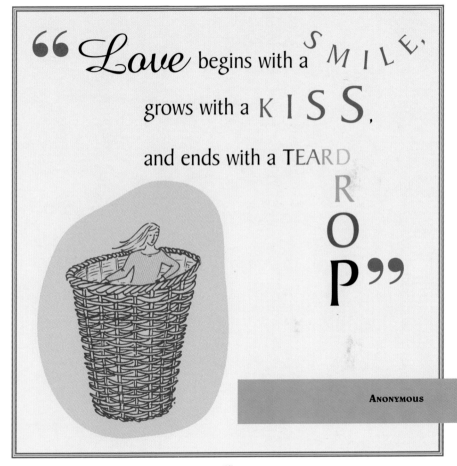

"*Love* begins with a SMILE, grows with a KISS, and ends with a TEARDROP"

ANONYMOUS

27

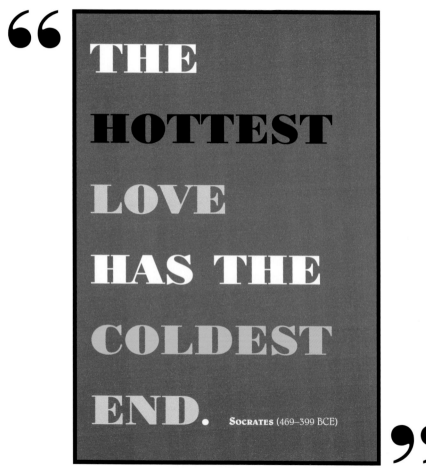

“

THE HOTTEST LOVE HAS THE COLDEST END.

SOCRATES (469–399 BCE)

”

"Nothing matters

matters

very much

and few few few few

things

matter at all."

The Chocolate & Cashmere Survival Guide to Break-ups

> **"A BREAK-UP WOULDN'T BE SO HARD TO TAKE IF IT WERE COVERED IN CHOCOLATE."**
>
> **ANONYMOUS**

So, you've done it—he's history. You were brave, you were strong, and you tried to be nice. But now you're discovering that being right can be pretty hard sometimes—so, in times of trial, these tried-and-tested tips will help you recover your poise.

1 Be kind to yourself. Crying buckets over a rat is not a contradiction—life is nothing if not confusing. Who would have thought, for instance, that well-educated, stylish fashion editors would regularly revive the puffball? Now, that is a worry.

2 Eat well. When in doubt, stick to the four basic food groups—chocolate cake, chocolate pralines, chocolate assortments, and the classic family-size slab.

3 Pay attention to appearance. Well-cut and comforting basics in delicious velvets and heavenly 4-ply cashmere jerseys will boost your confidence and maximize the chic of your tragedy.

4 Oh, and was that man this cozy and yet still exciting? Congratulate yourself on the realization that your sweater behaved better to you than he did.

5 Focus on the future. Every woman alive has had the "take one bite and sneak it back in the box" moment (or two). But rest assured in the knowledge your perfect 70% truffle is out there.

" I never met a piece of chocolate I didn't like. "

ANONYMOUS

"*Chocolate is way cheaper than a shrink and you don't need to book in advance*."

ANONYMOUS

"CHOCOLATE IS NATURE'S

WAY OF HEALING A BROKEN

H.E.A.R.T".

ANONYMOUS

" *Ever* *has it been*

that love knows not

its own *depth* *until the*

hour of **SEPARATION**

KAHLIL GIBRAN (1883–1931)

"

When one door of happiness closes, another opens; but often we look so long at the closed door that we do not see the one which has been opened for us.

HELEN KELLER (1880–1968)

"*Love* must be rein♥ented."

ARTHUR RIMBAUD (1854–1891)

Chapter 3

No
Regrets

?

SUITING THE CRIME TO THE PUNISHMENT...

When British wife Lady Sarah Graham-Moon found out her husband was philandering, she took action. Finding his collection of 32 Savile Row suits, she chopped a sleeve off each of them. Then she tipped a can of fresh white paint over his glossy blue BMW (which she located outside his mistress's home). Returning home, she assessed his wine collection and carefully left the best bottles of vintage claret on doorsteps round the neighborhood.

She said she regretted it. The neighbors didn't comment, though.

" REGRET is an appalling WASTE of energy . . . you can't build on it; it's only GOOD for wallowing in. "

KATHERINE MANSFIELD
(1888–1923)

"MEN?

Sure, I've known lots of them.

But I never found one I liked well enough to marry.

Besides,

I've always been busy with my work.

Marriage is a career in itself and to make a success of it you've got to keep working at it.

So until I can give the proper amount of time to marriage,

I'LL STAY SINGLE. "

MAE WEST (1893–1980)

RELATIONSHIPS

> **Relationships** are like glass. Sometimes it's better to leave them **BROKEN** than try to hurt yourself putting it back together.

RELATIONSHIPS

ANONYMOUS

The heart was made to be broken.

66 *I pay very little regard... to what any young person says on the subject of marriage. If they profess a dis inclination for it, I only set it down that they have not yet seen the right person.* 99

JANE AUSTEN (1775–1817)

66 *When a girl steals your man, there is no better revenge than to let her keep him.* 99

ANONYMOUS

"A New York
D I V O R C E
is in itself a diploma
of virtue. "

EDITH WHARTON (1862–1937)

> **He** *taught* **me** **house**keeping; *when* **I** *divorce,* **I** *keep* *the* **house.**

ZSA ZSA GABOR (1917–)

Chapter 4

MOVING

ON

" LIFE can be wildly TRAGIC at times, and I've had my share. BUT whatever happens to you, in the FINAL analysis, you have got NOT TO FORGET to laugh. "

" There is a time for DEPARTURE

even when there is no certain place TO GO. "

ANONYMOUS

FORGIVENESS does not change *the past*, but it does enlarge *the future*.**"**

PAUL BOESE (1668–1738)

back back back back back

> **Though no one can go back and make a brand *new* start, anyone can start from now and make a brand *new* ending.**

ANONYMOUS

start start start start start

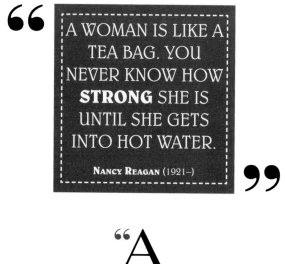

> A WOMAN IS LIKE A TEA BAG. YOU NEVER KNOW HOW **STRONG** SHE IS UNTIL SHE GETS INTO HOT WATER.
>
> **NANCY REAGAN** (1921–)

> "A SMILE *is the beginning of peace.*"
>
> **MOTHER TERESA OF CALCUTTA** (1910–1997)

> " *Life is lived in the present.*
>
> *Yesterday is gone.*
>
> *Tomorrow is yet to be.*
>
> *Today*
> *is the miracle.* "

ANONYMOUS

" Always forgive your ENEMIES – nothing a$n$$_n$$o$$_y$s them so much. **"**

OSCAR WILDE (1854–1900)

" TOMORROW I WILL MAKE MY OWN SO TODAY DON'T MEAN A THING. **"**

ANONYMOUS

The **GREATEST** healing therapy is *friendship & love.*

HUBERT H. HUMPHREY (1911–1978)

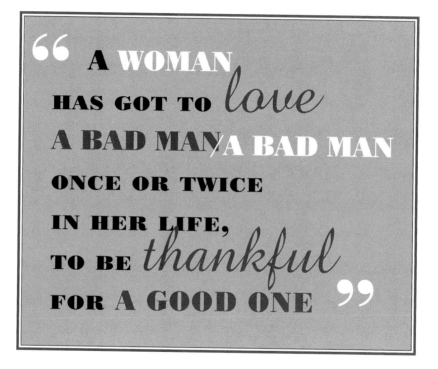

" **A WOMAN** HAS GOT TO *love* A BAD MAN/A BAD MAN ONCE OR TWICE IN HER LIFE, TO BE *thankful* FOR **A GOOD ONE** "

MARJORIE KINNAN RAWLINGS (1896–1953)

"The WEAK can never forgive. Forgiveness is the attribute of the **STRONG**."

MOHANDAS KARAMCHAND GANDHI (1869–1948)

" The ultimate lesson all of us have to learn is unconditional love, which includes not only others but ourselves as well."

DR ELISABETH KÜBLER-ROSS (1926–2004)

" THEY THAT SOW IN TEARS SHALL REAP IN JOY. "

Psalms 126:5

Seven Affirmations...

1 Every day brings new hope. The world keeps turning, the sun keeps coming up, and the rhythm of the seasons continues. Indeed, soon the new collections will be delivered to your favorite store ridiculously early. Always worth hurrying in to catch the best stuff, eh.

2 You have gained valuable life skills and successfully mastered the spiritual arts of forgiveness, grace, and serenity.

3 You have also mastered the extensive rules and regulations surrounding the activities of a little-known sports team. Well, this may prove useful someday. Who knows? Every day from now on will bring surprises.

4 You understand that every experience has value, enriching you and helping you grow.

5 Within reason, that is. You will never again have to

a face his "unique" gene pool—or rather, swamp—at family gatherings
b lie convincingly about that shirt
c listen to "the next big thing" as next door's dog howls for mercy
d run out of wash gel while actually in the shower.

6 You may have lost a man, but you've got yourself back—and a better, wiser, stronger version.

7 Someone out there is secretly hoping to meet the new, extra-special version of you.

> **"I NEVER hated a man enough to give him his diamonds BACK."**

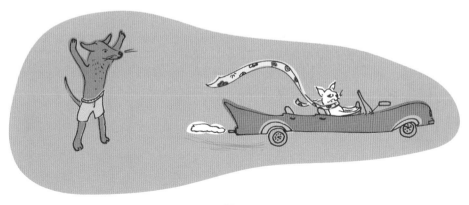

SOURCES AND ACKNOWLEDGMENTS

The publishers are grateful for permission to reproduce extracts from works in copyright.

p. 12 Dorothy Parker: "Comment", copyright 1926, © renewed 1954 by Dorothy Parker, edited by Marion Meade. Used by permission of Viking Penguin, a division of Penguin Group (USA) Inc.

p. 35 Helen Keller: Courtesy of the American Foundation for the Blind, Helen Keller Archives. Used with permission.

p. 52 Nancy Reagan: From address given to US Women's Congress, quoted in the Observer, London, 29 March 1981

p. 52 Mother Teresa: From *What Mother Teresa Taught Me*, copyright © 2007 by Maryanne Raphael, reprinted with permission of St. Anthony Messenger Press, 28 W. Liberty St., Cincinnati, OH 45202

p. 56 Marjorie Kinnan Rawlings: From *The Yearling*, Copyright © 1938 by Marjorie Kinnan Rawlings. Copyright renewed © 1966 by Norton Baskin. Copyright assigned to the Norton S. Baskin Revocable Trust of 1992

p. 57 Mohandas Karamchand Gandhi: From "Interview to the Press" in Karachi about the execution of Bhagat Singh, published in Young India (2 April 1931), reprinted in Collected Works of Mahatma Gandhi Online Vol. 51: www.gandhiserve.org/cwmg/cwmg.html Reprinted with permission of the Navajivan Trust

Every effort has been made to contact copyright holders and acknowledge sources, but the publishers would be glad to hear of any omissions.

INDEX
of
AUTHORS